Houseboat

*Reflections of North America's Floating Homes...
History, Architecture, and Lifestyles.*

Ben Dennis/Betsy Case

Smuggler's Cove Publishing
107 West John Street
Seattle, Washington 98119

ISBN 0-918484-00-6
ISBN 0-918484-01-4 pbk.

Library of Congress Catalog Card Number 77-2404.
Printed in the United States of America.

Author: Betsy Case
Author/Photographer: Ben Dennis

Book and Cover Design: Ben Dennis, Ray Braun, Bob McPake
Typesetting: Debbie Higgins
Production: Ray Braun, Debbie Higgins, Jansi Whitley,
            Paul Kotz, Bob McPake, Sue Johnson, Lou Buren, Jr.,
            Eric Savage, all of The Design Team, Seattle, WA
Copy Consultants: Rosemary Roraback, Jansi Whitley
Color Separations: Artcraft Colorgraphics, Seattle, WA
Printing: Kingsport Press, Kingsport, TN

Grateful thanks to those who opened
their doors to us, our cameras, and our notebooks.
And to the owners who just weren't far enough
along in their building or re-building . . .
maybe we'll catch you next time.

Houseboats reflect the spirit of their owners . . . more than any other dwelling since man discovered caves. The history of houseboats is a history of people. A hard-working, free and easy group of people who have a 'live for today' attitude and a love of the water. They have survived freak wind and snowstorms, lost moorages, sinkings and never-ending fights with the law. Yet they hang on . . . in the most unexpected places. Nestled at the foot of Manhattan Island. Moored in the heart of Seattle and Vancouver, B.C. Tucked into sun-speckled bayous near Pierre Part, Louisiana. In the midst of Sausalito's 'hip' culture. Houseboats reflect a hedonistic Great Gatsby lifestyle, a homespun simplicity, a mellow oneness with Mother Nature. They create envy in the hearts of us confined to the stability of land. They reflect a colorful past and hope for the future . . . . But most of all, they reflect their people.

Houseboat History

When you say 'houseboat' in Seattle, you think 'Terry Pettus.' Journalist. Champion of the Floating Homes Association. Confirmed houseboater for thirty-three years. His stories reflect Seattle's houseboaters. Their past. Their present.

When asked about Seattle's first houseboater, he pauses, lights the ever-present pipe, and answers, "As far as we know historically, a river pilot by the name of Rodney Allback was listed as living on Lake Union in 1904. 'Course we don't know about any earlier ones . . . census takers in those days didn't prowl around the lake trying to find characters living on houseboats."

Around the turn of the century, the first Yesler cablecar opened up Lake Washington to the people of Seattle. Houseboat summer homes dotted the shores. They were big, elaborate homes with seven rooms plus bath. Some became permanent dwellings for the 'jet setters' of the day, young marrieds of substantial income. As a matter of fact, most of the history of these boats is recorded in the society pages. Of course, they had some pretty shady neighbors. Take John Considine. He was a theatrical producer who amassed quite a fortune running crib houses. Actually, his real claim to fame was shooting and killing the police chief in a good old-fashioned shootout.

When the ship canal was cut between Lake Washington and Lake Union, most of these luxury homes went out of business. The lake dropped 8 feet . . . what used to be water suddenly became land. And if there's anything a houseboat needs, it's water under it. Then came economic pressures and the cry of pollution. By the end of World War II, houseboats on Lake Washington had virtually disappeared.

"During the Depression, the houseboat colony on Seattle's Duwamish River flourished, for obvious reasons. Living on the river was cheap. Fishing was good. It was a better way to live. IWW members, or Wobblies, worked in the mills along the river and were houseboat dwellers in great number. They'd leave the boats on a Saturday night to have their say at Pioneer Square's free speech corner. They were good . . . could even talk against a Salvation Army band. I got to know several old Wobblies . . . like Slim O'Neil. We'd sit all night and talk over a nickel cup of coffee. Slim and his friends would talk about their beats in the warehouse district. When labels came off the cans in warehouses, the cans were thrown away. Slim and friends picked 'em up for the next meal. Only problem was, you never knew whether it was going to be cling peaches or baked beans. But what the hell, it was free.

"Duwamish River houseboat people have disappeared today. Fred Strom is the last of 'em. He's eighty-six now, and lives on the Duwamish River waterway, just waiting for the Port of Seattle to evict him. The Port is going to build a barge terminal on Strom's land, where his boat has been moored for fifty years. He cooks on his hundred-year-old stove and lives with his cats, Hooligan, Useless, and Bismark. All he really wants

Ben Dennis

Terry Pettus.

Left: A vintage 1909 boat still floats on Seattle's Lake Union, now headquarters for a boat rental business.

out of life is to be left alone . . . but he's going down as the last houseboater on the Duwamish. This is the end.

"Lake Union is the last haven for houseboaters in the Seattle area. The houseboat neighborhood sprang up when the Denny Mill opened. But the Alaska-Yukon Exposition in 1909 really changed the character of the lake. It was a Seattle World's Fair . . . a hoopla to benefit Seattle. The boosters who wanted to do something good for the community trotted down to the state legislature and asked them for money. You can bet all the 'cow' counties were elaborately disinterested in voting money for a Seattle jamboree. So the boosters talked the legislature into selling private plat lots around the perimeter of the lake. That's a significant part of Seattle houseboat development. Actually, all the houseboats today are moored on private property. I can't imagine houseboats being moored on this lake if it wasn't private property.

"Even when the first houseboats were moved into the lake, there was a real mixture of people . . . working class people who were paying something for moorage. These people liked the water, liked the environment. There were city councilmen, lawyers, doctors, a chief fire marshall. Considerable more variety then than now. Probably a holdover from Prohibition days.

"During that time, there were a fair amount of places selling booze. It's harder to get a bottle now than it was then. You'd just call your bootlegger and he'd make a home delivery. Kitchens had trapdoors in case of a raid. People say this is the most glass-bottomed lake in the world.

"The mix of people changed again after World War II. Servicemen came home and bought houseboats. I think they didn't want to do a damn thing except bask. They were out there in their bare feet, painting their places with a feeling that there was going to be a better, kinder world. It caught a spirit of the time."

One young Marine had a short-lived houseboat experience. The night after he shoveled out his down payment on a $7000 houseboat, he was awakened by a geyser in the middle of his bedroom. He salvaged his uniform which he no longer needed, and clambered ashore, but the houseboat went down at its moorings. He was unscathed after many troop ship voyages in the Pacific, but wound up being sunk in a houseboat on the serene shores of a lake.

"Of course, the thing we're always battling around here is City Council. There was the problem of raw

University of Washington Library

sewage. The townfolk don't seem to realize that the houseboats only put about 1% of the raw sewage into the lake. But the Lake Union Floating Homes Association took the stand that any avoidable pollution is too much. As far back as 1937, there was talk among City Council members about 'removing houseboats from the shorelands.' Seems to be a cycle. One day when they don't have anything to talk about, they'll say 'Geez it's a good day to talk about getting rid of houseboats.' After years of fighting City Hall and consulting with engineers, the Floating Homes Association came up with a simple, efficient way to run plumbing and sewer lines from shore to boat. Now we get calls from as far away as Florida, asking for help with the same problems."

Of course, houseboating has other unique problems. The wood logs supporting them get soggy and boats slowly start to sink. Originally, more logs were rolled under the existing raft. Some houseboats had as much as fifteen feet of logs under them. In the fifties, air-filled drums were used to buoy up the floating homes. A team of two young divers named Bert Salisbury and John L. Metscar sank into the muddy gloom of the lake, put drums under the boats, and filled them with air. Bert remembers the day he met Terry Pettus:

"We were working on his boat in a windstorm. It was a nice day, but the wind was brisk. We moved his house out to the end of the dock and then decided to turn it around. It got caught sideways in the wind. It was acting like a sail. We couldn't get the boat in. It just kept drifting miles away while we held onto the lines. We were laughing like crazy . . . we'd pull and pull and get it close enough to the dock and then start laughing again. Then Terry's wife came out. They'd been having an afternoon beer, didn't even know what

was going on. She didn't realize the boat was loose. She kept feeling around for the gangplank with her feet and couldn't find it. We'd get the line in, look at her feeling around and laugh even harder . . . and away we went." The boat was finally secured without Terry or his wife knowing they'd been in danger of drifting out to sea.

After the problem of staying afloat was solved, there was the question of getting heating oil to the homeowners. The answer was the Tiny Tanker. Two of them, the *Dagwood* and the *Blondie,* were started by Harold Wolfe who says, "They weren't much. They had what passed for a pilot house and a couple of full oil drums forward." The Tiny Tankers were sold to houseboat owner Torbert Hull. He says newcomers to the houseboat scene laugh when they first see the *Dagwood*

Seattle's 'jet setters' settled on Lake Washington in the late 1920s.

'Father Time Whittled Away A[...]

Logs Collapse; Old Houseboat Nearly Sinks

New uphea[...]

BY CHARLES RUSSELL

A tired old houseboat took a dip in Lake Union yesterday and police rushed to the rescue in response to a series of frantic calls for help.

The houseboat, home of Mr. and Mrs. Harney D. Linam, partially sank at its moorings, 2768 Westlake Ave. N.

One side of the four-room houseboat settled into the [wa]ter when supporting tim[bers] attached to two float[s] collapsed and the huge [log]s popped out from under[nea]th the structure.

[NE]IGHBORING house[bo]at dwellers at the moor[ing]e, below the span of Au[ro]ra Bridge, said the water [is] 25 to 30 feet deep there. [The] Mr. and Mrs. Linam, at [h]ome with their two dogs [a]nd two cats, took their own [p]redicament calmly as the [f]loor listed to starboard and [the] water poured in.

But they needed furnitu[re] movers. And they need[ed] them pronto.

Neighbors called pol[ice] and soon crisp comma[nds] were going out over [the] police radio recruiting pa[-] trolmen to move furniture.

[...]disputes go back to 1968, when the county began [loo]king down on the appearance of the swelling [house]boat community. Houseboat residents quickly [...]d to inspections of their dwellings and fought [develop]ments bitterly during the early 1970s.

[In 197]2, the state Water Quality Control Board [ordered] all houseboats to stop dumping sewage over[board, to] hook up to a sewer system or put in holding [tanks. Man]y houseboats — those at George Kappas' [Harbor, 6]½, 22 at Yellow Ferry Harbor and 11 at [...] — tied into the shore sewer lines. [...]mitted a master development plan in 1970.

Portage Bay Lowered

HOUSEBOATS ARE RESTING on mud in Portage Bay, and waterline along shore is receding daily, leaving a path of drying mud in wake of continued warmth and lack of any ap[-]

FOR SALE

Seattle Post-Intelligencer
16 S Wed., Nov.

Houseboa[t] Will Be Restored

THE OLDEST floating structure in the Seattle area was moved across Lake Union yesterday on its way to restoration. The 50 x 100-foot houseboat was built in 1902. The houseboat was originally [use]d for a boat rental busi[ness] at Leschi Park. The [house]boat was moved to [Lake] Union in 1925. New [owner] Dick Wagner and [wife] [Ly]nn will share it. [Lynn], sculptor, will live [there] and will have a [...] [an]d studio. Wag[ner] [...] the low[...]

HOUSEBOAT FIRE—The Coast Guard and Seattle firemen poured water on a fire which virtually destroyed one houseboat and damaged two others yesterday after-noon. The fire, of undetermined origin, started in the home of Mrs. Pearl Phillips, 2606 Fairview Av. N., and spread to the other houseboats before it was put out.

Fire Razes Lake Union Houseboat

Fire of undetermined origin yesterday virtually destroyed a houseboat at 2606 Fairview Av. N. and caused extensive damage to two other houseboats. No one was injured.

The fire broke out in the home of Mrs. Pearl I. Phillips. Neither she nor her daughter,

Donna, 16, was at home.

The flames spread to the roofs and sides of houses occupied by James Melton, 2608 Fairview Av. N., a University of Washington student, and Mrs. Alex Maalea, 2504 Fairview Av. N.

The fire was brought under

control in about 30 minutes by firemen from Engine Companies 22, 7 and 17, Ladder Company 3 and a Coast Guard fireboat.

The fire was reported by Jimmy Brown, 12, of 2341 Eastlake Av. N. and John Fuller, 12, 2625 Boylston Av. N.

Removal Asked Of Houseboats In City 'Street'

(This is the third article in a series about Seattle's houseboat colonies, which Dr. Frank M. Carroll, city health commissioner, says "must go.")

In the newest twist in the dispute over ousting Seattle's 600 houseboats from their lakeshore moorings, the Board of Public Works is considering a demand that eleven houseboats be moved from a city "street" which is entirely under water.

[...] Bay Improvement

Water-Borne "Landmarks" Have To Go

[ON]E OF SEVERAL groups of house-[boats on the] shores of Lake Union which must [move for] private construction, causing sor-[row or conste]rnation among the occupants, some of whom are owners, other[s renters. This] flotilla parallels Fairview Ave. N. [between] Roa-noke and Edgar Sts.

Houseboat "IDAWIS" on Lake Washington. Furnished Comple[te]
Call North 664, or East 84

[...] on the star-board side.

"It's older than Methuse-lah," said Linam, surveying the houseboat. "Old Father Time has been whittling away at her with a scythe." The Linams, who estimated [$3,000,] moved

—(Post-Intelligencer Photos by [...]

or *Blondie*. But when they need heat on a frosty morning, that's something else again.

Like any other home, houseboats have their particular hazards. Pettus says with a grin, "When fishermen come through the ship canal after the season, they're celebrating and not navigating very well. Once in a while a houseboat gets in the way and a fishing boat slams against the dock. Our neighbor got hit several times. Finally he hung a flashing red light on his boat.

"Houseboat docks are also a hazard to drunks. On our first moorage, there was a lady who lived right at the end of the gangplank. It was a ten-foot wide gangplank without a rail. Ten feet, you know, would give any sober person a reasonable amount of negotiating room, but if you get loaded you might need more than that. They claim that lady was psychic. No matter what hour of the night, she'd hear a splash, grab a boat hook and out she'd run. The keeper of the gate . . . she lived there 18 years and never lost a customer. There's a saying, you know. The first time you fall in you're a houseboater. The second time you're drunk.

"Then there was Charlie. He was in his seventies, he lived just across from us. He had papers for everything, a shipmaster for all seas. Boy, could he drink! He'd dry out at sea. And was he a packrat . . . couldn't resist auctions. His boat was just like a tunnel. There was just enough room for him to fuss around in that

Seattle Times

little kitchen, a couple of places to sit, his bunk, and the rest was crates. Everything from boxes of bed sheets to a mimeo machine. We'd ask him, why do you buy all this? He'd say, well it was at an auction and you don't go to an auction unless you buy stuff. One night, Charlie was walking home from the tavern and got hit by a car. Doctors didn't think he'd survive. But he showed up a few months later at our front door in his robe and slippers. He had a cab driver in tow and said he needed a drink. He damn near emptied the fifth before he gave the bottle back. Charlie was determined to go back to sea . . . went down to the union and the doctors there said he couldn't even stand watch in port. But he kept trying and ended up with a quartermaster job. Said he knew he was gonna die sometime, but wanted to take one more cruise.

"Charlie was a good neighbor. Houseboaters have an unwritten rule that you don't visit unless you're invited. That's what makes this kind of life possible. People still maintain a warm relationship, even the new people on the lake today. It's impossible not to know your neighbors . . . every houseboat moorage is its own community.

"People on the lake have changed. It seems there are more children. Most of 'em learn to swim very young. Parents figure the water isn't any more dangerous than a busy street. One youngster even learned his first word on the dock . . . 'quack.' Today's houseboaters have a higher income. They're young married, professional, better educated. They're doctors, teachers, professors, advertising executives, urban planners. They don't need a prestige address and can have a bit of a bohemian lifestyle. I knew one man who was climbing the corporate ladder. He finally had to move because his address might wipe out his chances of being executive material. Some people still think it's wine and roses . . . or pot and roses. Houseboaters have evolved from low incomes to high incomes. A class has replaced a class."

But people on houseboats still have something in common. They love the life. There are no lawns to mow, folks are friendly, you can fish from your back porch and tie your sailboat up to a cleat on your deck. And sooner or later, all of Seattle floats past your living room windows. "People live on the lake as a way of life, there's no other answer. Besides . . . " Pettus pauses to rekindle his pipe, then smiles . . . "when you're on a houseboat dock, you're in God's pocket."

Cooks, loggers and camp bosses line up for a formal group picture in one of British Columbia's secluded floating villages.

The usual feeling of 'community' found on house-boat docks is intensified in British Columbia's floating logging camps. These floating villages house loggers, wives, cooks and playful groups of life-jacketed children.

At the beginning of the twentieth century, whole neighborhoods were afloat. Everything the loggers needed was on rafts . . . homes, hotels, general stores, cook houses. The remote villages were reached by boat, and all supplies were towed in. An early lady logger moved to the tiny inlet of Poet Nook with her sewing machine, wood stove, chickens and a pet canary all stacked on a barge.

Original floating villages were inhabited by men only. However, the hungry loggers became disgruntled with burned bacon and biscuits, and women cooks were imported. The food was better, but as one logger put the problem, "I'm not sure it's worth having to get cleaned up for dinner."

Romance blossomed and the female cooks became wives and housemothers to the loggers. In Seymour Inlet, two-hundred-fifty miles from Vancouver, the wife of a logging camp owner feeds and takes care of eight burly loggers. Mornings start at five-thirty. Meals are huge affairs of meat, potatoes, fresh bread and dessert. And the only reason for going ashore is to get soil for vegetables and flowers that grow in numerous buckets, barrels and boxes on the houseboat decks.

Life is an adventure in the float camps that dot the inlets of British Columbia. The children don life jackets for a boat ride to school. Radios keep communication fairly constant. The newest form of transportation from the city is a float plane. And 'cars' are streamlined fiberglass power boats. There is no television, but as one worried mother puts it, "If I had TV on during the day, I wouldn't be able to hear the children when they fall in the water."

Today, Canada's floating villages are a vanishing breed. They started with hundreds of communities along the coast. Now it is estimated that there are between a dozen and fifty left. They are giving 'way to housing developments and larger logging operations that build

Entire families settled down to the day-to-day routine of logging camp life in Western Canada's floating neighborhoods.

Houseboat villages thrived during Vancouver's depression days.

instant suburbs along the shore.

Fishermen like Angelo Sarcia were original members of the Vancouver houseboat population. Sarcia sailed around the Horn from Genoa in 1894 aboard a German ship. It was his first trip to America. Friends ashore persuaded him that it was the land of plenty, so in Seattle he left ship with $13 in back pay, traveled up the coast to visit friends in Vancouver, and never left. His first house was built on a raft and moored in Vancouver Harbour.

The houseboat population grew with the city until the Depression, when the colony mushroomed. An opportunity to beat the housing shortage, the dollar shortage and the tax collector attracted many out-of-work Canadians.

The largest colonies were concentrated along the shores of False Creek. Coal Harbour Colony was known locally as 'Shaughnessy Heights,' after a wealthy residential district, because Coal Harbour boats were the only ones with pumped water and electric lights.

A city survey in 1938 revealed certain houseboat statistics: "Population ever-growing. More than two hundred houseboats at present. Some four-hundred-fifty adults and one hundred children. No sewage facilities. Few direct water connections. Only seventy-seven light connections. Remarks: the people contacted seem contented and happy, most of them expressed satisfaction at living on the waterfront and a desire to remain there. There was apparently no sickness anywhere!"

Even though houseboaters were happy, the Vancouver City Fathers were anxious to be rid of them. Sewage facilities were 'improper,' the city couldn't collect revenues for water and electricity, and the houseboaters used schools and hospitals without paying taxes. Even the Truant Officer who forced houseboat children to class wasn't subsidized by floating families!

A floating hotel north of Vancouver was home away from home for transient loggers in the thirties.

The battle continues. Houseboaters today are still fighting City Hall . . . trying to erase the 'slum' image of Depression days, the forties and early fifties. Designs for proper hook-ups have been submitted to the city. A Floating Homes Association has been formed. Recently, a two-story suite of offices built on a barge was opened on the Vancouver waterfront. The floating offices are completely equipped with lifesaving gear and dinghy. And the staff members spend their lunch hours behind a fishing pole. An elaborate plan for a new Coal Harbour community was also recently formulated by two university students. The plan would include one-hundred-eighty new two-story houseboats, landscaped walkways and an 'adventure pool' for the children. It seems acceptance of the floating homes concept is coming.

No firm decisions have been made, pro or con . . . houseboat owners in Vancouver, like houseboat owners everywhere, are ready for a fight. According to a spokesman, "We don't really want to fight City Hall. We want to set up an organization that will have committees to work on problems like safety and sewage. We are all prepared to pay taxes. We're not just a bunch of hippies." They're airline pilots, librarians, playwrights, painters and engineers, sharing the ever-present harmony of the houseboat dock. "What appeals to me most is the honest-to-God friendliness. We have a real sense of community you won't find ashore. When I lived in an apartment, I ignored my neighbors and hated the land-lord. Here, all the neighbors are friends and I hate the marinelord!"

A Coal Harbour boat owner sums it up — "We're not just living here to beat the high cost of living, as so many people think. We like it here. It's our way of life and our way of beating the grind. We will pay our taxes and put in holding tanks . . . then we want to be left alone."

Missionaries on the Mississippi.

Right: Espanto, medicine man.

A twisting shell-covered road leads you to a lonely houseboat sitting on the tideflats of the Gulf of Mexico. Joseph Cheremie, with a big smile and a Louisiana Cajun accent, welcomes you aboard. Shrimp nets hang from every corner. New-born puppies scramble under crab pots to hide from strangers. Joseph and his wife have retired to their boat to relax and fish . . . "Everything we want to eat, we got it here, except beef." As you sip coffee fragrant with chicory, you notice a ship's wheel on the cabinet just under the coffee pot.

The houseboat is powered with a small engine, to 'high-tail it up the Gulf' when a hurricane hits. The Cheremie boat is modern, with the exception of a French armoire carved lovingly from cypress and probably handed down through generations.

Back in the Louisiana bayous, drifting lazily under moss-draped cypress trees, is another kind of houseboat . . .

remnants of adventurous shantyboat fleets that traveled the Mississippi in the late 1800s. They came from St. Louis, St. Paul and points north. They came to New Orleans and the lure of 'carnival,' following the ghost of Huck Finn. Mississippi shantyboaters had their own community traveling with them . . . preachers, medicine men, and just plain neighbors.

In an old frock coat and long black braids, Espanto the Mexican Indian Medicine Man went down the river selling his remedies to young and old. His boat was a traveling billboard proclaiming the potency of his wares. During cotton harvest one year, he took in over a thousand dollars in ten days. He was making his fortune 'til the town doctors got the marshall after him. The charge? Practicing without a license. Espanto gave the judge one hundred dollars cash for bail . . . then went back to work and made the hundred dollars up the same morning. The Mexican Indian Medicine Man finally retired from the river. That's when his friends discovered his real name was Billy and he was from Michigan.

The religious ills of the shanty dwellers were cured by people like Preacher John Robert Hames, who started as a Bible peddler on the Mississippi. Then he turned to itinerant preaching in the early 1900s. For thirty-five years he spread the Word, limping on his game leg that was shot in a gang fight. "Seven men jumped me, they did. They took my specs, what little money I had and tore my new suit off my back. Before running out, as they left, one of 'em shot me in the leg. They never expected me to fight, but I did. We certainly had a merry time for a while."

Louisiana houseboaters display the same kind of carefree attitude shared by waterdwellers all over the world. They like to fish from the living room if the spirit moves them. And when moving day comes, the usual bother of packing the china and calling a truck just isn't necessary. "I wouldn't want to live in one place all the time, not me," explained Claiborne Landry, after towing his two-room houseboat from Little Grand Bayou to the Dugas Canal in St. Vincent, Louisiana. "It's impossible to get sick of life, you just pull up stakes and move." The Landrys are in the moss gathering and fishing business, so it's handy to live close. Accompanying Landry, his wife and their children, were their next door neighbors, who decided to make the move, too. Says Mama Landry, "It's good to have another family nearby, if I need to borrow a cup of flour."

Mrs. Annie Simpson is another Louisiana houseboater who displayed little concern for the elements. After a storm tore her boat loose from moorage in Demory Hill, she just drifted out to sea. Two months later, rescuers found Mrs. Simpson thirty miles from shore in the Gulf of Mexico, calmly cooking up a batch of ham and eggs.

Except for four sophisticated new houseboats moored precariously in the New Orleans Ponchatrain Canal, houseboats are a thing of the past in Louisiana. Says Joseph Cheremie, "Used to be a lot of houseboats, but people went to something better. Me, I wouldn't have anything else. I sleep so quiet every night."

Brought in parts around the Horn from the East Coast in 1870, the Vallejo *ran between San Francisco, Mare Island and Vallejo until 1948. Since the early fifties, it has housed a colorful collection of water dwellers near Sausalito's Gate Five.*

Houseboat history in Sausalito has been colorful, confusing and, at times, downright riotous—from gala parties on lantern-bejeweled pleasure boats anchored near Belvedere in the late 1800s, to the War of Waldo Point. And for years, the color swirled in great gusts around the ferryboat *Vallejo* with Jean 'Yanko' Varda at its nucleus. Varda, a painter, was a romantic water gypsy, a lover of life and ladies, a personification of the free spirit found in Sausalito's houseboat community.

Friends remember 'Yanko' sitting at the edge of San Francisco Bay in a shocking-pink sweatshirt and paint-spattered pants. "He was eating wine-soaked strawberries and romancing a pretty girl." The *Vallejo* was his 'palace' . . . and his sheer joy for life lingers on in every part of the ark colony. He was a world renowned painter and friend of Henry Miller, contemporary of Picasso. His last twenty years were lived on the *Vallejo*, a one-hundred-year-old ferryboat which spent most of its life on a routine run between Mare Island and Vallejo. The *Vallejo* was originally purchased by artist Gordon Onslow-Ford, who shared his quarters with Varda. When Varda moved aboard with his tubes of paint and vibrant collages the routine ended!

To get better light in his studio, early one morning Varda and a few friends turned the *Vallejo* one-hundred-eighty degrees. This left Ford looking at the dock, while Varda got up each morning to spectacular Bay views. Ford finally had enough of this hilarity and moved. After he left, his walls were found covered with mattresses . . . this was his last futile attempt to stop Varda's noisy enjoyment of life!

In the late 1950s, Onslow-Ford sold his share of the *Vallejo* to Zen philosopher Alan Watts. Dr. Watts, a prolific lecturer and writer, interpreted Eastern philosophy and religion for the Western world. He often referred to the *Vallejo* as his oyster—"rough and homely on the outside, a rare treasure within."

Watts and Varda were fast friends, even though at times months went by without a meeting. During these years the *Vallejo* saw spectacular parties! Two-hundred-fifty people at a time were caught up in the celebration of the moment. There was wine, bread, cheese, fruit, spiced lamb, music, dancing—and color. Especially color! The rich colors of Varda's painting and sculpture, the brilliant costumes of his handmaidens, the flamboyant cushions and sails of his own sailing ship, the *Cythera*.

Jean Varda

Jim Kean, San Raphael Independent Journal

Ben Dennis

A turn of the century Belvedere houseboat now rests in the San Francisco Maritime Museum. Interiors have been restored to their original opulent condition.

Houseboating In North America, 1906

A houseboat in San Francisco Harbor.

The *S.S. Vallejo*, now owned and operated by the Alan Watts Society for Comparative Philosophy, is still cradled in the mud at the foot of infamous Gate Five in Sausalito. Under the peeling paint it is a proud monument to Alan Watts, Jean Varda, a multitude of friends, and a continued celebration of a water lifestyle.

California homes on the water began as early as the late 1800s, when a glittering colony of 'arks' floated in Belvedere Lagoon. Many were the pleasure crafts of wealthy San Franciscans, before the great earthquake. Each spring was heralded by the opening of the Corinthian Island Bridge, when thirty or more boats were towed from winter quarters to a summer resting place in front of the San Francisco Yacht Club on the Belvedere shore. Decked out with lanterns and pots of flowers, the arks floated happily under the stately gaze of Mt. Tamalpais. Families spent the week aboard the arks, while San Francisco's doctors, lawyers and bankers commuted to the city aboard speedy motor launches.

Boats like the *California,* an imposing craft with an eighteen-foot social hall, six staterooms and furnishings of Golden Oak, intermingled with small 'bachelor' boats. Young male owners of these boats also spent days in the city, but managed to relax on evenings and weekends by rowing over to court the daughters of nearby floating families.

Sporting the straw hat and white frock fashions of the day, a group of young California socialites row out for a lazy afternoon on the deck of a Belvedere ark.

San Francisco Maritime Museum

A long-extinct Alameda houseboat colony at the turn of the century.
Right: The City of Seattle, *a sidewheel ferry on its run between Seattle and West Seattle in the late 1800s. She now is a floating home in Sausalito.*

In 1906, San Francisco was besieged by earthquake and fire. Burned out of their mansions on Nob Hill, many ark owners moved to their water homes while the city was being rebuilt. The disaster didn't diminish the San Franciscans' appetite for socializing, however. The *H. J. Corcoran,* a restored ferry, served elaborate meals to members of San Francisco's 'Jolly Tars.' Membership of this elite club included bankers, lumber barons and stockbrokers. They lunched daily on mock turtle soup, fricassee of lamb, prime rib, kingfish, new potatoes and assorted fruits.

The Depression brought an end to lavish entertaining aboard the Belvedere arks. Many of them became year-'round rent-free homes for the impoverished.

After World War II, the Belvedere Land Company developed the Lagoon where the arks were protected. Many were demolished. Others were moved. Fate has scattered the survivors. One is now a Belvedere teen center. Another was donated to the San Francisco Maritime State Historic Park as a museum piece. Several can be found, still on barges, lining Belvedere's Main Street . . . spending the remainder of their days as gift shops and restaurants.

The houseboat colony on Larkspur Boardwalk

sprouted around 1915. The mainstays of this community were fishermen and retired ferry captains. The floating homes lasted until 1967, when the state repossessed the land for a flood control project. Seventeen boats were bulldozed and destroyed. A few boats survived. Today, they are pulled up on private land and protected by a strong community group.

Sausalito's Gate Five had humble beginnings as a mud flat where barges were repaired in 1914. The first houseboats were owned by employees of the Arques Shipworks. They patched barge hulls during the day and lived near their work at night. Gate Five was one of the original gates of Marin Shipyard, where Liberty ships were built during World War II. Men and women from the East Coast, the South and the Midwest passed through those gates . . . thirty-eight thousand of them. Very few were native sons. The locals left under the onslaught of 'foreigners.'

To construct the shipyard, the original Waldo Point on Sausalito's Richardson Bay was removed, creating a waterfront cove. To the eventual dismay of county officials, a perfect home for houseboats was also created.

After the war, the locals returned. The shipyard came under the leadership of Donlan Arques, son of the original owner.

When the San Francisco Bay bridges were opened, three magnificent old ferries were retired. Arques bought the *Charles Van Damme,* the *San Rafel* and the *Issaquah* for one-thousand dollars apiece and beached them at Gate Five, thus contributing to today's patchwork of ferries, scows and barges.

Arques wrenched the machinery from the *San Rafel* and donated it to a museum. The *Charles Van Damme* became a restaurant for awhile, then a gathering place and studio for young artists. The *Issaquah* sits beached with a broken back. They were joined in the early fifties by the *Vallejo* and *City of Seattle.*

Stacks still protruding, wheels now immobile, these ferryboats were the real beginning of Sausalito's present day houseboat colony. They are landmarks reigning over Gate Five and a quarter-mile of floating homes.

Gate Five became Haight-Ashbury-on-the-water in the early sixties. It was a haven for the discontented sons and daughters of America's middle class. It was also a home for artists who wanted to work without the daily hassle of a nine-to-five job.

Even today, scows sitting on the mud, tugboats, barges topped with domes and trailers . . . they are all connected by a merry mishmash of logs, ship's planks and whatever else can be found to constitute a dock. Most of the boats were built by their owners, starting from scratch. A community junkpile heaped with lumber scraps, window panes and furniture is the beginning of many Gate Five homes. A community shower has been built for anyone without running water . . . and that includes at least half the inhabitants.

Gate Five still attracts hundreds of young artists. Painters, sculptors, seamstresses, poets and carpenters have found the time and freedom to create. Many of them display their creations at 'Waldo Works,' the community gift shop.

A young sculptor named Christopher Roberts left his mark on the Gate Five scene in the early sixties. He was intrigued with the idea of turning houseboats into works of art. His first project began on one of Sausalito's many balloon barges—anti-aircraft boats anchored off Mare Island during World War II. His balloon barge project, shaped a bit like a Chinese junk, still floats . . . now the home of artist Shel Silverstein.

Chris began building his sculpture around existing shapes. A crane barge inspired him to design a big bird . . . and the *Owl* was born, built from the top down! The last, and most well known of Roberts' work was the *Madonna and Child.*

He went to work on this magnificent undertaking in 1969. The project was to soar sixty feet in the air from a base on an old piledriver. During construction, Roberts received a stop work order from the county, due to the absence of a building permit. He calmly explained that the *Madonna and Child* was a sculpture. One doesn't need a permit to build a sculpture. The unfinished *Madonna and Child* mysteriously burned on winter solstice in 1974. One resident describes the fire as "glorious and frightening . . . there were so many small boats moored in its shadow." Nothing else burned, but soon after the fire, Chris Roberts left his houseboat sculptures in Sausalito and moved on.

The Gate Five kaleidoscope of people and architecture is almost constantly under siege. In 1971, Marin County officials condemned thirty boats. Their efforts to remove the first five 'substandard' boats resulted in the Battle of Richardson Bay. Authorities boarded a small Boston Whaler, glided into Gate Five and towed a converted lifeboat hull belonging to artist Russell Grissom,

Hickinbotham Bros.
Construction Division
Stockton, California

United States Army
Balloon Barges
Contract No. W-2782-tc-5

September 1, 1943
V. Covert Martin

Barges built to anchor anti-aircraft balloons during World War II are now floating homes in Sausalito Harbor.

out to sea. Grissom returned home to be told, "Hey man, the authorities just ripped off your boat." Members of the houseboat community formed a naval convoy consisting of Chinese junks, canoes, rowboats and tugs . . . and took off in pursuit. During the standoff between the motley Gate Five fleet and the authorities, Grissom and his boat were forgotten. He spent the night aboard and the next morning moved back to his mooring.

Due to the constant threat of county authorities, the face of Gate Five is changing. After trying for fourteen years, the Arques Shipyard has obtained necessary permits to start building new docks and renovating old ones. Houseboats moored at nearby Gates Six and Six-and-a-Half are already up to code. Plans include four new docks and reconstruction of a fifth. There will be an addition of three-hundred-fifty new berths. Efforts will be made to keep every boat now moored at Gate Five . . . but they will have to hook up. Those who can't afford moorage fees will have to sell or move on to new locations.

One of Gate Five's earliest residents describes the change—"It all started with a bunch of drunken plumbers during the war, then the artists moved in . . . now the rich people have discovered the lifestyle."

A floating photography studio in Portland's Scowtown.

A contemporary riverhouse on Portland's Willamette River displays colorful bits and pieces of salvaged materials . . . a throwback to the building habits of early 'river rats' in Portland's Scowtown.

A waterborne architect and his son have decorated their river home with rescued railroad signs and turned posts from a Victorian home. In the early 1900s, equally resourceful Scowtowners created planting boxes from discarded barrels and less-than-sturdy gangplanks from driftwood.

Scowtowners were members of one of the country's largest houseboat colonies at the turn of the century. Charter members of the colony were loggers. But they were soon joined by a fascinating mix of characters . . . the dispossessed son of a British Lord. A seamstress who was once an heiress. Telephone girls. An entire crew of firemen.

According to early recollection, Portland's first houseboats were on the water for a very short time. The Great Flood of 1894 stranded two boats on a bank near Upper Scowtown. The river rats decided they liked solid ground as much as the river, and settled down to life as landlubbers.

Portland's three settlements—Upper, Middle and Lower Scowtown—were located at the foot of Mill Street,

under the Burnside Bridge and near the Madison Bridge. The Burnside Bridge settlement was ordered to move in 1906, to make way for new mill wharves.

The population of the settlement was always changing . . . a fight with your next door neighbor could be ended abruptly, just by pulling up anchor and floating away to a new moorage. Scowtowners lived rent-free and faced few dangers. Drunks were an occasional hazard, especially when they had to be fished out of the river! And river swells were the other cause for concern. An early wedding ceremony was interrupted when a giant swell broke the cable on a scow. Preacher, bride and groom took an unplanned honeymoon trip down the Willamette.

The addition of another colony further up the river near the North Pacific Lumber Mills once caused the comment, "There are five hundred scows on the Willamette and at least five thousand people" . . . an average of ten people per scow!

Scows were joined at the turn of the century by the houseboats of Portland's wealthy. Even though many of the scows were neatly painted and ringed by white picket fences, they couldn't compete with the luxury of these fashionable vacation homes. Between April and September, Oregon's scenic rivers were crowded with

Houseboat and tenders on the Willamette River.

1907 Sunset Magazine

the houseboats of lawyers, doctors, architects and businessmen. Many of the boats were powered, cruising up and down the river to enjoy the view. Others were anchored near Ross Island, two miles from Portland.

One vacation home, the *Tic-Tiac,* was a big surprise for first-time guests. Outside, she looked like an ordinary scow. Inside, her owners had furnished her with gleaming Oregon Fir. The *Tic-Tiac* belonged to a young couple who used her for year-'round entertaining . . . even in winter months, they would row out for Sunday afternoon teas aboard.

Entertaining on a more lavish scale was done aboard the *Raysark,* an eighty by twenty-eight foot boat with six staterooms, a three-ton ice chest, a bathroom with running water, a darkroom and an awning-topped deck. As many as one-hundred-fifty guests per weekend crowded aboard the *Raysark,* and the annual Fourth of July celebration was renowned throughout the Pacific Northwest. In 1903, a few select friends were invited to join the *Raysark* on a maiden 'voyage.' She was towed from Portland, over the swirling waters of the Columbia River Gorge, through the Government Locks to a

From the late twenties to mid forties, floating homeowners flourished in Portland's Lower Scowtown.

summer home near Lyle, Washington. A one-hundred-seventy-eight mile excursion, just to find 'picturesque' surroundings!

Remnants of Portland's riverhomes survived the usual pressure from City Hall and the cries of pollution. New moorages were opened in the early '40s. Carter's Moorage was built in 1945 on the Oregon Slough, and during the first few years, Mrs. Carter recalled, "Beavers swam by and chewed on the log rafts. But we cleared the land, put in gangplanks and pilings, and charge a monthly moorage. Just like in a trailer court." Like

houseboaters around the country, they only had two real problems, "Floods and falling in."

Scowtown is now waterborne suburbia. Hooked-up boats cling to the shores of the Willamette. Some things, however, remain constant . . . the same high spirits enjoyed by early river rats. The delight at having no lawn to mow. The mystical feel for the water. According to a present-day river dweller, "Living on the water is a mysterious experience. The river has so many moods and I feel comfortable on it."

A family portrait on the shores of the Willamette.

On the East Coast at the turn of the century, houseboaters could follow a decorating scheme laid out in the book *Houseboating in America*. Fashionable owners were advised that a "bright, clear, pea green has been found the most desirable color for the galley and servant's quarters." Leaded glass was by far the most acceptable for windows. Fireplaces were suggested to keep homes warm and comfortable, even in wet winter months.

Most East Coast houseboats were merely summer retreats and had but one major problem . . . The Domestic. It seemed to be an accepted fact that "the independent maid would hardly consent to a position on a houseboat unless she were a most extraordinary person!"

The housecleaning problem was solved by Charles Moyer, a New York City naval architect. His 26 foot 'bachelor' boat was built in 1904. It was large enough for comfort and an occasional overnight guest. But small enough to keep housekeeping chores to a minimum.

The regal splendor of Mrs. Payne Whitney's boat *Captiva*, however, must have called for a certain amount of upkeep. The 110-foot diesel powered boat contained a formal dining room furnished with matching sideboards, ornate hand-carved table and chairs. After a gourmet dinner, Mrs. Whitney's guests could relax with brandy and a cigar in a carpeted parlour, looking through a wall of windows to a nautical view. The *Captiva* was completed during the early 1900s. It was immediately put into service, transporting Mrs. Whitney and her passengers from the New England Coast to the upper Hudson River . . . just in time for the racing season at Saratoga.

Further down the coastline, the *Nordene* had the honor of being one of the first water homes on the Potomac after World War II. A sub chaser during the war, the *Nordene* was sailed by Captain and Mrs. John Conway from Spain through the high seas of the Atlantic to a berth in the shadow of the Washington Monument.

Even the Midwest has made a contribution to the nation's houseboat population. In the winter of 1952, Fred Bissell started work on a 'country chalet' tied up on the Mississippi near Dubuque, Iowa. His interior decor was an interesting combination of class and clutter—from rattan chairs and a pot-bellied stove to a Tiffany lamp fished out of the river.

Shantyboat preachers, retired sea captains, footloose artists and upstanding citizens of the community have all been houseboat owners across America . . . they were and are a hearty group. For over one-hundred years, they have braved hurricanes, floods and human storms stirred up in the city council. They have emerged from a colorful and sometimes questionable past to a hopefully secure future of up-to-code moorings and respectability. Yet they are all linked—hooked on houseboats. Terry Pettus sums it up . . . "We're captives of a joyous way of life."

Houseboat on Kootenay Lake in the early 1900s.

Houseboating In America, 1906

Houseboat Flotation

Houseboat flotation is as varied as the boats themselves. Many are boats in themselves . . . ferries, surplus balloon boats, landing crafts, tugboats.

The first houseboat flotation was probably a simple wooden raft. The best examples of this could be found on the many lakes and rivers of the Pacific Northwest in the late 1800s. Large cedar logs, sometimes four and five feet on the butt end, were strapped together. Seasoned snags from forest fire areas were considered the most desirable logs. The fire dried and sealed the normally porous cedar, making it into a perfect flotation material. Some Lake Union boats still float securely on logs cut from the slopes of Queen Anne Hill and Capitol Hill in

Seattle. When one layer of logs became waterlogged, another layer was rolled underneath in an inverted pyramid form. An older boat could be resting on as many as twelve to fifteen feet of cedar logs! And, a recent sign on the waterfront announced that these same logs are selling for $3 a foot. Since the logs are preserved indefinitely in fresh water and could be resold for lumber, many houseboaters are actually floating on their investment!

In the 1950s, as cedar logs became scarce, steel drums were used as supplemental flotation under the logs. Divers worked in the murky waters of Lake Union to maintain and fill the drums with air.

In other parts of the country where timber was less plentiful, resourceful water dwellers designed their homes atop scows and barges. Moored in fresh water, the scows and barges lasted decades. In salt water however, wooden flotation was besieged by torredos and other wood-eating water inhabitants. And, there was only one salvation against having your barge eaten out from under you — hauling it out of the water each year and coating it with copper paint.

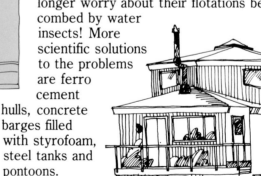

Many houseboaters, having lost the battle of the torredos, once again turned to innovative ideas. Today, several California houseboats rest serenely on pilings high above the water. Their owners no longer rock with the waves. But, they also no longer worry about their flotations being honeycombed by water insects! More scientific solutions to the problems are ferro cement hulls, concrete barges filled with styrofoam, steel tanks and pontoons.

Houseboat Architecture

Houseboat architecture encompasses ideas that range from the height of elegance to the ultimate in funk. The end goal, however, is the same — a tight ship where every corner counts.

"Every crack and crevice should be used for something," according to master craftsman Bob Blackford, who has been designing and building Sausalito houseboats for twelve years.

Blackford's boats are magnificent . . . filled with stained glass, hand-crafted wood and the best things money can buy. "I try to give my customers something unique, something no one else has." He does everything by hand, and "it takes forever."

The curve of a satin-smooth handrail and the perfect fit of molding against floor tells you that Blackford loves his work. "Being near the water gives me great pleasure, and building houseboats is a combination of work and pleasure."

Blackford believes there will always be a market for his boats . . . luxurious water homes like the *Pirate,* a tugboat renovated and sold for two-hundred-fifty thousand dollars, and the *Taj Mahal,* complete with swimming pool and elevator.

He thinks the future looks rosy for Sausalito houseboats in general, and his houseboats in particular. "If you build a work of art, you can always find an art collector."

Jim Jessup, a Seattle houseboat architect, has created floating homes that capture the space economy of a sailing sloop and the charm of earlier Lake Washington boats.

When Jessup designs houseboats he "designs for delight!" His boats are a myriad of multiple levels and light-filled corners. A houseboat owner since college days, he spent a short time on land but found that "being away from houseboats was very boring."

The addition of new boats to Seattle's Lake Union added a certain respectability, according to Jessup.

However, he thinks the day of the new boat is almost over. "Boat moorage is going up fast. Codes restrict the building of larger boats. No moorage is being planned. There won't be too much new building . . . there's just no place to go."

Jessup has worked on twenty new boats and six renovations. Now his designs are being used on shore. "Today you need more casual, relaxed spaces. People like the spirit of my designs, and they don't have to be on a houseboat to enjoy it."

A freestyle form of houseboat architecture is practiced by David Wright, a woodcarver. With little knowledge of building or codes David and his wife built a boat from the bare necessities up. "We started with a tub, refrigerator and all the basics, then we started cutting. First, we made holes in the walls and put in windows. Then we put a hole in the ceiling and moved everything up!"

But Wright's advice to houseboat builders follows a familiar pattern: "Most boats are small, so design things to fit in small spaces." If you're building your own boat and you're poor, he suggests finding a moorage surrounded by driftwood. "All the wood in our boat was free — walls, stairs, shelves!"

His boat has been built and re-built many times. "You reach a point where you can't think of anything else to do." Tentative plans are being considered for another boat. "My next boat won't have a flat roof. I'll design eaves, so the rain will run off. Now, we seem to have leaks every fall. I'll also put some round shapes in . . . I like round shapes. But, you have to learn to build something square before you build something round!"

His final piece of advice has appeal for the experienced architect as well as for the houseboater who has done nothing more than repair the gangplank. "What really counts is getting the job done right . . . and designing spaces that live in harmony with the water."

"I've so loved my houseboat and my boat Nargoorek, *that when I shuffle off this mortal coil, I've made arrangements for some of my cronies to lay me out in state on the Nargoorek cabin, pile cordwood around it, and saturate it with oil. Then I want it made fast to the old houseboat where I spent many a happy year, and towed out into Puget Sound and set afire. I don't want any mourning or tears. It is to be a happy affair. Nobody could have gotten more out of life than I have.*"

Jerome McLeland

French Cathedral windows, built at the turn of the century, are the heart of this boat. Special privileges come with its 'end' moorage. The best views. The biggest space for your wind surfer. But most of all, "being the last house on the dock contributes to your peace of mind . . . . Walking down the docks at night helps you lose the growls. And when you live at the end, you get to walk farther."

"I'll stay on the water always. Its moods constantly change. The fog lifts. The tides roll in. That's one of the beauties."
A carpenter and two seaworthy felines share a boat hidden alone in a tiny cove.

Sheer rock cliffs provide protection from the prevailing southerlys. Lofts have been added. Windows moved. Walls pushed out. "This boat, like the weather, is always different. I'm to the point where I'm moving the same spaces back again, without even realizing it!"

Long hours of work transformed an empty seine skiff into a "Chinese junk" home covered with hand-split cedar shingles.

The lifestyle is "far from the maddening city." Yet, the city is a mere block away.

"I wanted to build a new boat with the character of older boats." A houseboat architect designed seven contemporary levels around four rough-hewn cedar logs. "There's only one door in the whole house. I kept the spaces open and friendly, so you'd never get trapped away in the kitchen."

The boat shows off 'collectables' bought before construction was even begun: a 1914 fan with rosewood blades found in a Montana railroad station and a ship's telegraph sold 'by the pound.'

"On a houseboat dock, you retreat from the pressures of the world. When you walk down the dock at night, it's like going on vacation."

Lake breezes drift into the master suite through a porthole rescued from the aircraft carrier U.S.S. Bunker Hill.

Alone in a cove with evergreen surroundings, a young woodcarver and his wife picked a homesite where there was plenty of driftwood. "We didn't buy a stick of wood. And the wood we found on the beach was full of nails, so we got those free, too!"

"You just start cutting holes in the walls and putting in windows!" What was once an old wood hauling barge, then a neglected houseboat layered with red and black paint, blossomed after months of scraping and scrubbing. Plant garlands trail past stained glass and exquisite carvings . . . products of the tiny workshop in the bow of the boat.

"The work has been worth it. Building another boat would be fun. Life has a different rhythm when you're living on the water. You get to fish. And I love to fish."

"When the exterior was completed, we moved in with an ice chest and sleeping bags. The rest of the boat took two years to finish, a little at a time." Wood is everywhere. An old-fashioned dutch door design was modernized with the use of beetle-scarred pecky cedar. *"We bought the cedar because it was cheap at the time. Now it's the 'in' thing to use."*

"We like the activity of water life and so does Ho-Tei."
Raised on a houseboat, he grew up keeping a close eye on
dock neighbors, and an even closer eye on visitors.

A bedroom wall is lined with cedar shingles. An ancient brandy barrel holds the bathroom sink. Originally a sleeping loft, the master bedroom is now crowned by a skylight . . . "The sun wakes you up in the morning. And it's a lot nicer than an alarm clock!"

Sausalito's houseboat colony . . . bathed in the serenity of a sunrise.

A brass trimmed handmade stove had humble beginnings as a metal life buoy. It was cut . . . sculptured . . . and mounted on a porthole fitting by an inspired boat builder.

"I feel like I'm living in a childhood fort. I guess I took Peter Pan too seriously." "Retiring" to a home on the water, an ex-school teacher joined two cabins from the ribs of another boat. On summer's first warm day, she unceremoniously moves kitchen, complete with stove, onto the deck! Behind her casual mooring is her mini-farm . . . blooming with flowers, vegetables, goats and chickens.

Inspired by Balinese masks, Annie makes her own creations from paper mache. They stare fiercely down from the walls. And near her bed, a collection of neglected flea market dolls has found a new home.

Offset printing plates were recycled to create . . . a "houseboot!"

"A house on land is a nice place to visit. But I wouldn't want to live there!"

Canadian geese are expected guests on Seattle's Lake
Union and often drop in for dinner. But, a Vancouver
Island cougar? His occasional presence on deck is an eye
opener for afternoon sailors! The stuffed cat normally
decorates a corner of the houseboat living room belonging
to sportsman Bill Niemi.

A greeting card designer shares room and board with his houseboat cat . . . "She owns the place, I'm just a guest." There are no set plans for the boat, he just "does it as it comes."

"Most of the stuff in the boat is free. Some of the things I found . . . other things were given to me by friends."

A handbuilt redwood tub with urethane finish and a rain forest setting is a great place for bubbles and boats . . . or parties of "up to eight people at a time!"

"I had a chance to build my own thing on the water. I put in every nail myself. This boat is one-hundred percent ours!" Hovering over the surrounding houseboats, this one is perched on a supporting pedestal to catch the view.

Peg Leg Pete balances on his beam for a breakfast of fish bits . . . he'll have nothing to do with scraps and bread crumbs. A true gourmet bird.

A hand-carved column from a Victorian mansion finds new life in the midst of an indoor jungle. Initials and a tiny heart carved near the base are the remnants of an early romance.

*Transported in parts around the Horn from the East in
1870, this stately old sidewheeler ran between San Francisco,
Mare Island and Vallejo until 1948. Inside, the Vallejo
sparkles with the paintings and sculptures of her former
occupant, Jean Varda. Her exterior condition once caused
him to comment, "Ships are constantly trying to commit
suicide."*

Varda's bed, made from casting molds, still faces the sunrise on the Bay.

Dragons, puppets, and play costumes were designed for "play days," a new adult therapy developed by Vallejo occupant Mariam Saltzman to recreate the carefree magic of childhood.

On the shore end of the Vallejo, just outside the Alan Watts Society Head-quarters, a deck farm thrives.

Backlit bottles amid the stones give Varda's fireplace a translucent quality.

Vallejo *quarters are shared by young artists and poets . . .*
who celebrate sundown with a musical interlude on deck.

Driftwood walls are lifted from the ordinary by specks of original paint, some in three or four layers. "At first, I'd overlook the paint-spattered pieces. Then I got fascinated with the history that was behind them. Who knows where they came from . . . old fishing boats . . . river shantys." A grillwork bench folds on original brass hinges, to save space. Brass ship propellers are candlesticks. Grillwork from a ship's pilot house is the breakfast table. A nautical home, protected from the wind by shoji screens. "Backlighted by passing boats at night, it's really sexy."

"Cost was no object. We had a vision." An 1870 vintage tug spent the better part of its life working up and down the Sacramento River. Then men with a vision took over. Remodeling lasted fifteen months, beginning with an innovative idea: ferro cement applied over the existing wood hull. Cast iron stoves and crystal light fixtures were carefully restored. Interiors were creatively customized with hand-carved paneling.

Empty spaces below were transformed into a sumptuous master suite reflected in a ceiling of etched mirrors. Down the hall, past guest berths, is a sauna ringed by hand-painted Mexican tiles.

The cast iron stove is an 1890 Caboose original. The embossed bath pedestal is an original from the Pirate *herself.*

Marin County boats on a summer morning — as varied as the owners themselves.

"We saw the movie Houseboat . . . *and thought it was so neat, we went out looking for a houseboat the next morning. Within hours we discoverd the* Ameer. *It was fate, I guess."* Named after a Turkish title of nobility, when things Oriental were in fashion, the Ameer *was first moored in the Corte Madera slough near Larkspur. It was built at the turn of the century by a civil engineer. "It's a well-constructed ark. I guess that's why it survived."*

Blow torches were used to burn off layers of old paint. The captain's bunk was re-installed. Imagination and three years of hard work restored the Ameer to her former splendor. "We made our own personal changes, but we designed everything to look like an original feature of the boat."

*The art studio is surrounded by an 'antique advertising'
collection — old tins, comic strips, posters and billboards . . .
a sideline hobby of the* Ameer's *cartoonist-owner, Phil Frank.*

Houseboats and sailboats . . . they just naturally go together.

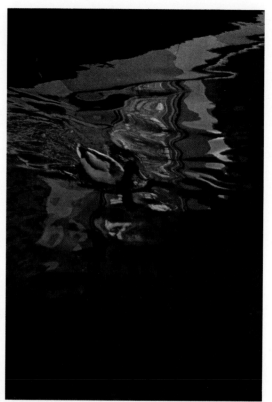

A birch tree rises gracefully from the living area through the roof, crowning a European-style floating cottage. The carpenter/owner painstakingly finished the exterior and is now remodeling the inside.

The bridge of the one-hundred-ninety-two foot battle tug
Jupiter Queen *was cut away from her deck, then barged to
Washington's Kitsap Peninsula. The World War II tug now
sits surrounded by trim lawns instead of stormy seas.*

The *Butterfly. A living space and a sculpture. Her first
level is almost waterlogged. Without new flotation, the*
Butterfly *could become an endangered species.*

Madonna and Child *temporarily changed the skyline of Sausalito's waterfront. Designed by Christopher Roberts, the masterpiece burned, but the Owl remains, a monument to his enormous talent and enthusiasm.*

"This is a beautiful way of living . . . a total dream world, a little piece of paradise. Where else would I get to fish off my back porch?" A giant clam shell from Kuai gleams in the bath. Carp imported from Japan swim lazily in a former hot pool, occasionally drifting over to suck your fingers in affection.

A renaissance chandelier is in reality a cyclone fence gate
run over by a truck. A collection of clear crystals turns it
into a free-form masterpiece!

Photo: Howard Bland

A model racing yacht presides over meals in the dining room—this is indeed a tropical island boat.

Houseboat whimsy.

Egrets search for small fish in the tidal shallows.

Innovative ideas in wood and stained glass are designed by an ex-advertising man who has re-channeled his creativity. His work is an imaginative addition to neighboring boats as well as his own.

Built during World War II in Stockton, California, this balloon barge originally anchored air-filled anti-aircraft balloons. The anchor ring still stands in the living area, an historical conversation piece. An old barn wall frames a bed/couch/pigeonhole desk combination that fits together like a jigsaw puzzle. Original portholes light up below-decks area—including the bathroom, where a four-foot toilet paper roll (you choose the color) is the "ultimate in hospitality."

Kids and water? The mix is a happy
one on this World War II landing craft.
The ever-present life jacket protects
them from an occasional tumble off the
deck. At night, the tides rock them to
sleep under the patchwork windows of
a "free form" geodesic dome.

A gallery of stained glass treasures includes a three-hundred-year-old St. Elizabeth, a tiny piece of real Tiffany, and escapees from a Pittsburgh urban renewal project. "We brought them home, carefully cut holes in the wall and had to reinforce the entire roof! It was a spur-of-the-moment decision, but that's what houseboating is all about."

"A magic and beautiful home" created from an old sidewheel ferry. A long working life started on an 1888 run between Seattle and West Seattle. Next, the Martinez-Benicia run in California. The Navy re-built her as a yard ferry in 1944. Now she sits in grand repose at the end of a dock.

Daylight slants through paddles of the original wheel.
A deck that once carried hundreds of working men is now
filled with plants and sunshine. The massive table supported
by an anchor winch is an invitation to leisurely dining, with
Elizabethan flair! A handmade sailboat is tied up outside,
for "drifting around the bay . . . speed is never the object."

The Hawaiian koa wood captain's bed is designed with extra storage. The koa wood couch fits snugly into a corner and cushions lift out for dining, Japanese style. "The necessities are all built in. You could move into this boat without a single piece of furniture!"

A talkative Cockatoo welcomes clients to the floating home offices of Rare Earth Real Estate in Sausalito.

Probably the only houseboat in existence complete with Video Beam and pool table! Birds and monkeys chatter in cages behind a desk made from an abandoned lapstrake canoe. The owner "tried to make it as much like a tropical island as possible."

Give an artist a paintbrush and anything can happen. "The shape of the boat was terribly dull, and I just couldn't afford to change it. I had to put something on the walls, so I started with the dragons, then painted waves on the decks and roof. My imagination just took off!"

The fine tradition of "tasseling" was started on this houseboat dock. When total privacy is requested, the tassels are hung out to alert dock neighbors.

Early "ark" decor of lace-trimmed pillows and overstuffed velvet chairs is topped off by kitchen cabinets made from the remnants of San Francisco's Pier 41.

A survivor of Lake Washington's houseboat era, this 1909 boat was a summer home moored at the bottom of a street-car line. Towed to Lake Union in the 1940s, she is now headquarters for a boat rental business and home for a family of four.

"The kids love to sail and swim. It just seems to come naturally, living in this environment."

Harbormaster's office and weekend retreat. A houseboat with an engine, and what an engine! Built in 1926 and sold as half of a pair to an Italian fisherman named Red, one engine went in his boat, the other in his sister's garage. Red lovingly fired up the stored engine once a year for almost fifty years. Then it was installed . . . shining and never before used . . . in this 1914 hayscow. Red the fisherman still drops by for an occasional visit with his engine.

"When you live on a houseboat dock, you're in God's pocket."